LUNDY ROCKALL DOGGER FAIR ISLE

A Celebration of the Islands Around Britain

Words by Mathew Clayton
Illustrations by Anthony Atkinson

EBURY
PRESS

1 3 5 7 9 10 8 6 4 2

Ebury Press, an imprint of Ebury Publishing
20 Vauxhall Bridge Road
London SW1V 2SA

Ebury Press is part of the Penguin Random House
group of companies whose addresses can be found
at global.penguinrandomhouse.com

Penguin
Random House
UK

First published by Ebury Press in 2015

www.eburypublishing.co.uk

A CIP catalogue record for this book is available
from the British Library

ISBN 9781785037795

Printed and bound by Clays Ltd, St Ives plc

MIX
Paper from
responsible sources
FSC® C018179

Penguin Random House is committed
to a sustainable future for our business,
our readers and our planet. This book
is made from Forest Stewardship Council®
certified paper.

'Compared to this what are cathedrals or the palaces built by man; mere models or playthings, imitations as diminutive as his works will always be when compared to those of nature.'

Joseph Banks on visiting the island of Staffa in 1772.

Contents

Introduction

'There are people... who find islands
somehow irresistible. The mere knowledge
that they are on an island, a little world
surrounded by the sea, fills them with
an indescribable intoxication.'
Lawrence Durrell,
Reflections on a Marine Venus

Caldey is a small island, owned by Cistercian
monks, that lies a few miles off the coast of
South Wales. It was here, in the 1920s, that
my grandparents met, fell in love and got
married. A branch of my grandmother's family
ran the island farm, and she worked there as
a milkmaid. My grandfather, Valentine KilBride,
was in Caldey working for the monks. He was
a weaver and had been brought to the island
to weave cloth to be made into habits.

Since then Caldey has occupied a special place
in my family's imagination; a carefree paradise
blissfully untethered from the modern world. In
1978, when I was ten years old, my aunt Jenny
took me there on holiday. It was a wonderful
few days. I remember scrambling down a cliff
path using ropes to get to a beach, being shown
a tablet in the church inscribed with the Ogham
alphabet, an ancient script in which each
letter corresponds with a tree, and at the
edge of a field behind the pond, we climbed up
an old apple tree, scratched off some moss and
found the initials my grandparents had carved

half a century earlier. Adventure! Mystery! Romance! I was enchanted.

There was something else about Caldey, something less tangible. Something about being in a place with such clear boundaries; where the land doesn't stretch off into the unknown. It may sound far-fetched but there was something about being on Caldey – and I have felt this on other British islands – that made me feel strangely secure. Maybe it is not that surprising. Islands have always been places of both escape and refuge.

There are hundreds of islands dotted round Britain, they are not so much the 'other' but 'another' – another version of Britain that runs in parallel, but out of sync with the mainland. Although they are many miles apart they have a lot in common. Monasteries, hermits, Vikings, smugglers, shipwrecks, lighthouses, pirates and seabirds are all regular features in island stories.

Being away from the hubbub of urban life also gives them a unique atmosphere. Without the noise of traffic you can hear birdsong more easily. Not being surrounded by buildings means you can see the sky, and without street lights it comes alive with stars each night. On islands without cars you have to walk everywhere and have more time to experience your immediate environment: the grass on which you walk, the sun and rain on your back. You are literally more in touch with nature and the elements.

A few years ago I spent New Year on Lundy, an island in the Bristol Channel. At midnight we stood in a pitch-black field as a storm raged around us. The rain fell like javelins, the wind threatened to whisk us away any second, and the sea, smashing into the rocks, sounded like the land under our feet was exploding. It was a magnificent sensory overload, very different to how I would have experienced the storm in a city.

The way we see the world is shaped not just by our direct experience, but by the stories we tell about it, and so we felt it was important to include some fictional islands in this book. They are often the lens through which we see real islands.

You may also have noticed that the title includes Dogger, a name you may recognise from the shipping forecast. This currently isn't an island, although it once was. Before the last ice age ended 6,500 years ago Britain was part of Europe, connected from Scotland right down to Cornwall. As the sea rose this area would have turned first into an archipelago before slipping under the waves. It is often referred to as a land bridge, but this is a misleading description as it conjures up an image of something small and thin connecting two larger pieces of land, whereas the land bridge actually covered an area larger than the UK. The earliest record of humans living in Britain is from 800,000 years ago, and we expect that humans lived in Doggerland for a long, long time, but really we have only just started learning about this lost land. It serves as a reminder that the shape of Britain is always slowly shifting.

Finally, an apology for the fact that we couldn't fit every British island into this book, but hopefully there are enough to get you slightly tipsy, if not fully intoxicated.

Mathew Clayton

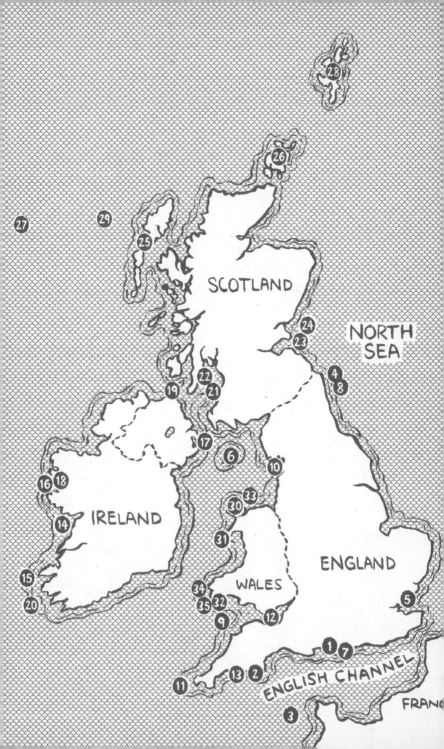

The Islands of Great Britain & Ireland

<table>
<tr><td>1.</td><td>Brownsea Island</td><td>21.</td><td>Ailsa Craig</td><td>27.</td><td>Rockall</td></tr>
<tr><td>2.</td><td>Burgh Island</td><td>22.</td><td>Arran</td><td>28.</td><td>Shetland Islands</td></tr>
<tr><td>3.</td><td>Channel Islands</td><td>23.</td><td>Bass Rock</td><td></td><td>Fair Isle</td></tr>
<tr><td>4.</td><td>Farne Islands</td><td>24.</td><td>Bell Rock</td><td></td><td>Foula</td></tr>
<tr><td>5.</td><td>Foulness</td><td>25.</td><td>Hebrides</td><td></td><td>Out Stack & Muckle Flugga</td></tr>
<tr><td>6.</td><td>Isle of Man</td><td></td><td>Colonsay</td><td></td><td>Papa Stour</td></tr>
<tr><td>7.</td><td>Isle of Wight</td><td></td><td>Eilach An Naomih</td><td></td><td>Whalsay</td></tr>
<tr><td>8.</td><td>Lindisfarne</td><td></td><td>Eilean Bàn</td><td></td><td>Yell</td></tr>
<tr><td>9.</td><td>Lundy</td><td></td><td>Eriskay</td><td>29.</td><td>St Kilda</td></tr>
<tr><td>10.</td><td>Piel Island</td><td></td><td>Flannan Isles</td><td>30.</td><td>Anglesey</td></tr>
<tr><td>11.</td><td>Scilly Isles</td><td></td><td>Jura</td><td>31</td><td>Bardsey</td></tr>
<tr><td>12.</td><td>Steep Holm</td><td></td><td>Lewis</td><td>32.</td><td>Caldey</td></tr>
<tr><td>13.</td><td>St Michael's Mount</td><td></td><td>Luchruban</td><td>33.</td><td>Puffin Island</td></tr>
<tr><td>14.</td><td>Aran</td><td></td><td>Rum</td><td>34.</td><td>Ramsey</td></tr>
<tr><td>15.</td><td>Blasket Isles</td><td></td><td>Skye</td><td>35.</td><td>Skokholm</td></tr>
<tr><td>16.</td><td>Clare Island</td><td></td><td>Staffa</td><td></td><td></td></tr>
<tr><td>17.</td><td>Copeland Islands</td><td></td><td>North Rona</td><td></td><td></td></tr>
<tr><td>18.</td><td>Dorinish</td><td>26.</td><td>Orkney Islands</td><td></td><td></td></tr>
<tr><td>19.</td><td>Raithlin</td><td></td><td>Hoy</td><td></td><td></td></tr>
<tr><td>20.</td><td>Skellig Michael</td><td></td><td>Papa Westray</td><td></td><td></td></tr>
</table>

English Islands

Brownsea Island

Burgh Island

Channel Islands

Farne Islands

Foulness

Isle of Man

Isle of Wight

Lindisfarne

Lundy

Piel Island

Scilly Isles

Steep Holm

St Michael's Mount

Brownsea

Brownsea is a 500-acre island in Poole Harbour that is one and a half miles long by three-quarters of a mile across.

It was the site of the first scout camp in 1907, described here in an issue of *Scouting* magazine:

The 22 boys who attended Brownsea Island camp ranged from 9-17. Thirteen were from upper-class families and attended such exclusive boarding schools as Eton, Harrow, and Baden-Powell's alma mater Charterhouse. The other nine were working-class boys from Poole and Bournemouth. They were selected by leaders of the Boys' Brigade, a youth organisation that featured marching, drill and military lore. Despite the sharp class divisions of Edwardian England, the boys got along well.

Years later, Arthur Primmer, who was one of the working-class boys, remembered: 'Here's something of the atmosphere there. One of the upper-class boys in my patrol put up his hand one day and said, "Please, sir, can I leave the room?" And one of the town fellows said, "Silly fool, doesn't he know he is in a tent?"'

Today the island attracts over 100,000 visitors a year. Part of it is leased to the John Lewis partnership, which operates a staff hotel in the old castle. There is woodland, heathland and even a lagoon. Wildlife includes red squirrels, sika deer and peacocks.

Burgh Island

Off Bigbury-on-sea
in Devon is Burgh Island.
Its first lodging was
a summer house built in
the 1890s by the music-hall
star George Chirgwin. He
was famous as the 'white-
eyed kaffir', a minstrel act
whose blacked-up face was
distinguished by a single
white diamond shape over
his right eye. He sold the
island to filmmaker and
industrialist Archibold
Nettlefold, who built
a beautiful art deco hotel,
that resembles a beached
ocean liner. The hotel is
still open today. It became
very fashionable in the
1930s; guests included
Edward and Mrs Simpson

and Noël Coward. Agatha Christie also visited, and used it as the setting for two stories, *Evil Under the Sun*, featuring Belgian detective Hercule Poirot, and the whodunit, *And Then There Were None*. Visitors can walk to the island at low tide, but at high tide require the assistance of a sea tractor, that looks like a rickety old shed on stilts.

Channel Islands

There are eight inhabited islands off the coast of Normandy with a population of 170,000. Victor Hugo described them as crumbs that had fallen

MOULIN HUET BAY, GUERNSEY

off France, and it is true that the Channel Islands are far nearer the Continent than England. But although some of the architecture looks European and the street names are in French, as soon as you step off the ferry you are in no doubt that you are in England.

The Second World War

The Germans took over the Channel Islands in June 1940 shortly after the British government declared them a demilitarised zone. The Nazis stayed for the next five years. The islanders had an uneasy relationship with their occupiers – many resisted (although never using firearms) whilst others collaborated to varying degrees. The islands' government's policy, taking their instruction from London, was that the inhabitants should passively co-operate. The Germans put the clocks forward by an hour and insisted that people drive on the right hand side of the road.

They also passed anti-Semitic laws and built four concentration camps on Alderney, which housed Russian, Jewish and European prisoners. Hitler was keen that the islands were well defended, and part of this plan was to build a vast network of underground tunnels in Jersey.

The British liberated the islands on 9 May 1945. A child from Jersey later described the scene: 'It was the most wonderful day of my life, we went down to the harbour and there were boats and ships and English soldiers were coming ashore. And people were laughing and crying and dancing and they had sweets and chocolates that they gave to us. We hadn't seen sweets or chocolates for five years.'

Bergerac

Bergerac was a very popular BBC detective series set on Jersey that ran from 1981 to 1991 regularly attracting audiences of over 10 million. Robert Banks Stewart created it after Trevor Eve decided he did not wish to continue with another Banks Stewart detective series, *Shoestring*, leaving the BBC with a gap in its schedules.

Broadcast on Sunday evenings, it starred John Nettles, playing the troubled detective Jim Bergerac, who had returned to the Channel Islands on the back of a broken marriage and an alcohol problem. He drove a red 1947 Triumph Roadster and most episodes featured his former father-in-law, a lovable rogue called Charlie Hungerford.

While much of the series was constructed as classic whodunits, often featuring people hiding a secret from their past, *Bergerac* did occasionally stray into weirder territory touching upon black magic and the myth of Atlantis. Such is its hold on the popular imagination that on a recent visit to Jersey someone would mention *Bergerac* to me at least three times each day. In 2013 the BBC announced it would bring back the series, but with a younger version of Jim Bergerac.

The Barclay brothers

Six miles east of Guernsey is Sark. Three and a half miles long and one and a half wide, it is divided into two parts linked by a high, thin ridge. It is Britain's last fiefdom, run by a seigneur who pays an annual rent to the Crown of £1.79p. In 2008 Sark held their first elections. The officials voted in were broadly in favour of the old system.

Not everyone was happy. The Barclay brothers, multimillionaire businessmen who had built a home on the nearby islet of Brecqhou, claimed there was 'no true democracy'. It was the latest salvo in a battle between the brothers and the residents of Sark. The Seigneur's wife Diana Beaumont commented, 'They were the ones that started all this democracy business, now they don't like it because they haven't won.'

20

Farne Islands

'Is there in the whole field of history, or of fiction even, one instance of female heroism to compare for one moment with this?'
Letter to *The Times*

On 7 September 1838, Grace Darling looked out of her bedroom window on the Longstone lighthouse and saw what she thought was a boat striking the Harcar Rock.

She alerted her father William, the lighthouse keeper. Through a spyglass they could see that three or four people had managed to climb off the boat and were clinging to the rock. William judged the sea to be too rough for the local lifeboat crew. If a rescue was going to be attempted he needed to do it – but he couldn't manage it alone. William and Grace set off in a 20-foot boat. As they rowed near the rock, it became clear that they had underestimated the number of survivors. Two trips would be needed. In the end they rescued eight men and one woman.

The newspapers picked up the story and Grace found herself in the middle of a media frenzy (William's role was forgotten). There were boat trips from Newcastle to see where she lived. Grace was bombarded with letters and requests for support. This took its toll on her health. In 1842, aged 26, she died of tuberculosis.

St Cuthbert

St Cuthbert was born in Northumbria in 635
and died in 687. His life spanned the transition
from paganism to Christianity in north-east
England. He moved to Inner Farne at the age
of 40 to live as a hermit. By then, he had spent
ten years as the abbot of nearby Lindisfarne.
He stayed on Inner Farne for a further decade.
While there he passed a law to protect the local
colony of eider ducks — one of the first ever
bird protection laws. He left Farne having been
persuaded to become a travelling bishop. He
spent two years in this role, before he felt that
his time on earth was ending. He returned to
Farne and died. He was buried at Lindisfarne,
but has not rested easily since then.

Eleven years later he was 'elevated' as part
of a ceremony to declare him a saint. His
remains were miraculously undecayed, which
was taken as a sign of holiness, and his grave
became a place of pilgrimage. In the 9th
century following Viking attacks the body was
brought to the mainland. In the 12th century
he was entombed in an ornate shrine in
Durham Cathedral (not before the coffin had
been opened once more). Rich visitors would
leave gifts, including the tusks of the Narwhal,
which were believed to be unicorn horns
and thus very magical. Further examinations
of his remains took place in the 1530s (when
a commissioner of Henry VIII broke one of
the legs), and then again in 1827 and 1899.

Foulness

Foulness is one of six islands that form an Essex archipelago. They are all low lying and are protected by sea walls, but are still prone to flooding. The Ministry of Defence has owned Foulness since 1914 and access to the island is restricted. Before the 20th century the only way to reach Foulness on foot was by the Broomway, a path that ran parallel to the coast up to half a mile from the shore (the sand nearer than this being too soft to walk on). In 1904 the author Herbert W Tompkins described why

this route is called The Broomway: 'Of the brooms there are nearly 400; they are placed 30 yards apart, and are sunk two feet into the sand. Every year they are renewed; but it is necessary to repair many of them at shorter intervals.' Over 100 people have died having lost their way and been caught by the incoming sea on this lonely, and often foggy, stretch of sand. The Wakering Stairs, shown here, are a headway, built over the softer sand, that leads out to the now unmarked path.

Isle of Man

The Isle of Man was invaded in the 5th century by the Celts, and again in the 9th century by Vikings. Eventually it formed part of a kingdom that stretched from the Orkneys, through the Hebrides and down to Man, ruled over by the Lord of The Isles.

The Celts left behind a language, Manx, a branch of Gaelic. The last native speaker, a fisherman called Ned Maddrell, died in 1975.

The Vikings left behind their form of government. The island's parliament the Tynwald has met since 979, and their laws are noticeably different to those of the mainland. The highest rate of income tax is 20 per cent and there is no corporation tax. A report on offshore tax havens in the *Guardian* in 2013 noted that there is a UK company registered for every two residents of the island.

And it is not just tax laws that are different. Birching, as a method of juvenile punishment, continued to be used up until the mid 1970s (it was abolished in the rest of the UK in 1948), and even then they didn't get round to scrapping the laws related to it until 1993.

PLEASE DO NOT CUMB ON THE WALL

Isle of Wight

'We are so delighted with our purchases; the grounds are so extensive, & the woods would be lovely anywhere, but going down to the edge of the sea, as they do, makes it quite a Paradise, added to which it is so private & we can walk about anywhere, unmolested.' Queen Victoria writing in her journal, Sunday 30 March 1845

The Isle of Wight is the largest English island. It was called Vectis by the Romans (although no-one can quite agree why). There are remains of at least seven Roman villas and it was known to be an important agricultural centre.

Roughly a thousand years later the Vikings arrived, did some pillaging and

burning, and then decided to stay – using the Isle of Wight as a base from which to pillage and burn other parts of southern England.

More recently in the mid 19th century Queen Victoria arrived and decided to build a home. Her husband Prince Albert designed Osborne House (see below) in an Italianate style. The royal couple made the island fashionable and in their wake Dickens, Tennyson and many others of a poetic and artistic persuasion followed.

Today the island is a destination of choice for tourists and yachtsmen. Less so for prisoners – there are two prisons; Albany and Parkhurst (that opened in 1805).

Lindisfarne

'AD. 793. This year came dreadful fore-warnings over the land of the Northumbrians, terrifying the people most woefully: these were immense sheets of light rushing through the air, and whirlwinds, and fiery dragons flying across the firmament. These tremendous tokens were soon followed by a great famine: and not long after, on the sixth day before the ides of January in the same year, the harrowing inroads of heathen men made lamentable havoc in the church of God in Holy-island, by rapine and slaughter.'
Anglo-Saxon Chronicle

Shaped like a frying-pan Lindisfarne is three miles long and one and a half miles wide. You can drive to the island at low tide across a causeway.

In 634 an Irish monk, St Aidan, sent from Iona in Scotland, arrived at Lindisfarne and set up a monastery. It became the centre of Christianity in northern England. Here one of the world's most famous illuminated books, The Lindisfarne Gospels, was produced, consisting of 259 richly decorated pages. The artist, according to a note at the back of the manuscript, is believed to be Eadfrith, the Bishop of Lindisfarne between 698 and 721.

Seventy years after Eadfrith's death the Vikings chose the island for their first proper violent foray into Britain, a decisive turning point in the history of Britain.

Lundy

Lundy is situated only 20 miles off the bucolic north coast of Devon, but it feels more remote and otherworldly. The coastline is mainly cliffs, 400 feet high in places, and there is only one safe landing point.

This has made it a perfect refuge for pirates and a cast of other ne'er-do-well eccentrics keen on keeping the outside world at bay. The island doesn't have many trees; the buildings stand austerely on their own.

There are two lighthouses, a domestic looking castle, an oversized church, a little shop, a smattering of grand and less grand houses and a fantastic pub, The Marisco Tavern, that never locks its door and has incredible views across the Bristol Channel. Since 1969 the Landmark Trust has managed Lundy, and the 23 houses available for rent now provide a perfect refuge for holiday makers seeking tranquility.

Shipwrecks

The *Jenny* was a ship with a crew of 30 and a cargo of ivory and gold dust travelling from Africa, when it hit rocks on Lundy in 1797. All but one of the crew died. Much of the ivory (but not the gold) was salvaged soon after. In 1957 a bottle washed up on the Devon coast. Inside was a letter written on 15 August 1843, which said, 'Dear brother, Please e God I be with y against Michaelmas. Prepare y search Lundy for y Jenny ivories'. No-one knows why the letter's author was still searching for the ivory almost 50 years after it had been retrieved.

The cliffs of Lundy have proved disastrous for many ships. The Old Light was finished in 1820, funded by a group of local merchants hoping to make the passage up the Bristol Channel safer. It was built on the highest point of the island, which proved to be its undoing. It was too high up; mists and clouds made it invisible to passing ships. It was decommissioned in 1897. Perching precariously halfway down the cliffs on the west side of the island, the Battery was a fog station built after it was realised that no ships could see the Old Light. The two ruined cottages (see opposite) housed the gunners and their families (reputedly at one time a family of ten lived here). The gunners' job was to fire blank charges from two cannons every ten minutes during fog. With the Atlantic swirling like a boiling cauldron all around, it is hard to imagine a less hospitable place to bring up children.

Piel Island

Piel Island is situated one mile off the Cumbrian coast. It covers roughly 50 acres and contains an impressively ruined castle and a pub, The Ship Inn. The castle dates back to the 12th century, when King Stephen gave the island to a Norman abbot so he could establish a monastery. The current building with its motte and bailey was constructed in the 14th century. It was during this time that the Abbot of Piel was caught engaging in some very unmonkish behaviour; smuggling.

It is rumoured that the monks built a tunnel connecting the island with Furness Abbey on the mainland.

In the 15th century Lambert Simnel and 2,000 German mercenaries landed at Piel with the intention of overthrowing the king, Henry VII. They were eventually defeated at the Battle of Stoke Field.

Following the Dissolution of the Monasteries the island passed through the hands of various nobles. At the start of the 20th century the current owner, the Duke of Buccleuch, in a very noble gesture gave it to the local town of Furness. The earliest record of a public house on the island is from 1800. The landlord is also crowned the King of Piel, a tradition that possibly dates back to Simnel's v time. The ceremony involves an old oak chair, a crown, a sword and a large quantity of alcohol being poured over the king's head. A visitor in 1813 noted that the island's only inhabitant was the king, and the loneliness of the job was 'apt to drive him to his beer-barrel for company'.

Scilly Isles

'So all day long the noise
of battle roll'd
Among the mountains
by the winter sea,
Until King Arthur's table,
man by man,
Had fallen in Lyonesse
about their lord.'
Alfred, Lord Tennyson

The Scilly Isles consists
of 200 islands and rocks
situated 28 miles south
west of Cornwall. They
were at one point
a single landmass, but
rising sea levels meant
they started splitting
apart around 4,000 BC.

It is also possible that even further back the Scillies were joined to Cornwall. In the 16th century Elizabethan antiquaries published stories of a lost land off the Cornish coast called Lyonesse that contained many towns and churches. The Seven Stones Reef that lies 7 miles off the Scillies was supposedly the remains of a town called the City of Lions. There are similar stories of a submerged land: the Lowland Hundred off Cadogan Bay in Wales, and Ker-Is off Brittany. The islands have been inhabited since at least the Bronze Age; evidence of Roman settlement has also been found.

Tresco Abbey Gardens
Augustus Smith leased
the Scilly Isles from
the Duchy of Cornwall
in 1834 and began
a lifelong
campaign to improve
their economy and tackle
widespread poverty. He
built a house on Tresco and,
around the old priory
ruins, began creating
a subtropical garden

that now covers 15 acres. Thousands of plants from 80 different countries, many of which wouldn't survive on the mainland, are arranged on a series of sheltered terraces. Alongside this is the Valhalla Museum that houses a unique collection of ships' figureheads, many from boats shipwrecked on the Scillies.

Steep Holm

Kenneth Allsop was a pioneering conservationist, television presenter and author who sadly killed himself in 1973. His friend the author John Fowles helped set up a trust in his memory after he died.

The plan was to buy Eggardon Hill, an ancient wood that Allsop had campaigned to save, but when that proved too expensive they turned to Steep Holm, a small island in the Bristol Channel.

In March 1976 they bought it for £10,000. The trust has run it as a bird sanctuary and nature reserve ever since.

Allsop was an interesting and complicated man, who wrote about the countryside but also published a book about American hobos. His most popular book, *In the Country*, was a compilation of his *Daily Mail* columns that attracted some criticism as he actually divided his time between West Dorset and London. If you want your heart broken read *Letters to his Daughter*, published posthumously.

In 1803 a wild peony, *Paeonia Mascula*, was discovered flowering on Steep Holm. Although common in China and the Mediterranean this was the first time it had been seen in the UK. For some years it was believed to be native to Steep Holm, but the current theory is that it must have arrived on the island with some Augustinian monks in the 12th century.

St Michael's Mount

'The most wonderful thing about the Mount is the way in which in all its parts man has co-operated with nature to produce a perfect and harmonious whole. As viewed from every point on the mainland it is difficult to determine where nature's work ends and man's begins.'
Thomas Taylor, historian, 1932

The Greek traveller Pytheas visited Britain in the 4th century BC. The original description of his travels has been lost but other writers quote him. Two of them mention an island called either Ictis or Mictis that lies near the coast and is the centre of the tin trade between Europe and Britain. Was it St Michael's Mount? Some people believe so.

More recently in the 11th century Edward the Confessor established a monastic cell on the island; putting it under the administration of the similar looking Mont St-Michel in France.

After the suppression of the monasteries the island eventually passed into the hands of the St Aubyn family; who managed to hang on to it for just under 300 years before they gave it to the National Trust.

46

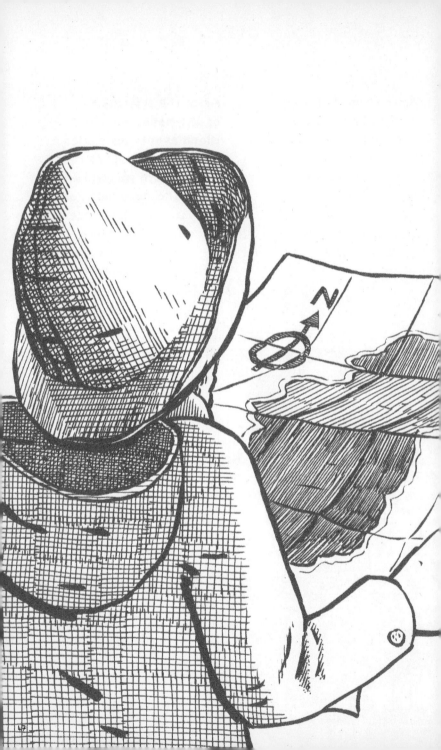

Irish Islands

Aran
Blasket Isles
Clare Island
Copeland Islands
Dorinish
Raithlin
Skellig Michael

Aran

Inishmore, Inishmaan and Inisheer are collectively known as the Aran Islands. They lie in Galway Bay off the west coast of Ireland. In the 1930s filmmaker Robert J Flaherty made a groundbreaking documentary, *Man of Aran*, about the daily struggle of life on the islands.

A large amount of poetic licence was used in the film: the family featured was not a real family, and their home was built specially. *Man of Aran* is strange and beautiful – as much about the terrible power of the sea as it is about the islanders.

Blasket Isles

The Blasket Isles, a group of six islands
off the south-west coast of Ireland, were
populated up until 1953, when the last 15
inhabitants were evacuated to the mainland.
Life was hard; they survived by fishing,
but there was no shop, no electricity,
and storms could cut the Blaskets off for days
at a time. It was not surprising that the first
attempt at evacuation had to be cancelled
due to bad weather.

The islands' influence though continues to
be felt through a series of books written by
islanders: over 40 in total, mostly recording
the life and folklore of this isolated place.
The three best-known authors are Tomás
Ó Criomhthain (pictured opposite), Peig Sayers
and Muiris Ó Súilleabháin. These writers were
encouraged by a number of academics who
came to the islands in the early 20th century
to study the Irish language.

Tomás Ó Criomhthain expressed a view of
his writing that could have been shared by
all of the authors; he wished 'to set down the
character of the people about me so that some
record of us might live after us, for the like of
us will never be again.' Tomás wrote two books,
Island Cross Talk, which was a compilation
of diary entries, and an autobiography, *The
Islandman*. One of his children, Seán, also
wrote a book describing the emigration of
the last people to leave the Blaskets.

Clare Island

Clare Island is one of supposedly 365 islands in Clew Bay on the west coast of Ireland. It is best known for a pirate queen called Grace O'Malley. Born there in 1530, her father having founded the island's abbey. She operated a protection racket – boats all along the Atlantic coast of Ireland were forced to pay her a fee to guarantee their safe passage. There are many apocryphal stories associated with her. In one, she is resting below deck, having given birth the previous day, while a battle rages above her on deck. Her captain comes into the cabin and tells her they are losing, and she declares, 'Can you not do one day without me?' – jumps out of her bed, grabs her pistols and helps them defeat a Turkish foe. In another, having seen her only son behaving like a coward in battle, she shouts at him, 'Are you trying to hide in my backside, where you came from?'. It is true, however, that in 1593 she managed to organise a meeting with Queen Elizabeth at Greenwich and persuaded Her Majesty to allow Grace to continue her piracy as long as it was restricted to attacking foreign boats. She died in 1603 and is buried in the Abbey. An inscription on her grave reads 'Invincible on Land and Sea'.

The Copeland Islands

Off the coast of Northern Ireland, on the southern side of the mouth of Belfast Lough, lie the three uninhabited Copeland Islands known individually as Lighthouse, Mew and Copeland Island.

Over a century ago there were at least 100 people living on them. Evidence of this can be seen in the 'lazy beds' that dot the landscape. These parallel ridges of land were used to cultivate crops (often fertilised with seaweed), and can still be found all across the Hebrides and the west coast of Ireland.

Today the islands are owned by the National Trust and managed by a group of amateur ornithologists who run a bird observatory in the old lighthouse keeper's cottage.

The islands are home to 4,000 breeding pairs of Manx shearwaters. They arrive each year in February and leave in July, travelling over 6,000 miles to South America, where they spend the winter. They are often seen gliding (or shearing) close to the waves, and to avoid predators only come into their nests at night. The tops of their body and wings are black and the underside is white. They form lifelong monogamous pairs and can live for a long time. In 2003 a ringed bird was found on Copeland that was at least 55 years old.

Dorinish

In July 1967 the Beatles set off for Greece. Their plan was to buy an island where they could live, away from prying eyes. After an acid-drenched cruise in a luxury yacht they discovered an island for sale that had a fishing village and four beaches (or four nearby islands, depending on who is telling the story) – one for each Beatle. The price was £90,000.

Due to restrictions in exporting currency buying the island was not straightforward, and by the time the legal issues had been sorted out the Beatles had lost interest in islands – all except John, who later that year spent £1,700 buying his own island, the 19-acre Dorinish, situated off County Mayo on the west coast of Ireland. Lennon moved his psychedelically painted gypsy caravan to Dorinish, but stopped visiting after his divorce from Cynthia. In 1970, he lent it to squatter and free festival organiser Sid 'King of the Hippies' Rawle. He established a commune on the island that lasted until 1972, when a fire destroyed their stores.

Just before he died, it is believed that John Lennon was enquiring about renewing his lapsed planning permission. But soon after his murder Yoko sold it for £30,000 and donated the money to an Irish orphanage. At the time of writing it is up for sale once again, with an asking price of 200,000 euros.

Rathlin

Rathlin is the only inhabited Northern Irish island. It was an important Viking stronghold: they arrived in 795, two years after they landed on Lindisfarne. In 1840 over 1,000 people lived there. Today, the year-round population is just 100.

On the seafront of Church Bay is a ruined warehouse, the last remnant of the kelp industry which was of great importance to many Scottish and Irish islands from the start of the 17th century up until the 1930s. Kelp is a seaweed that grows on the sunlit areas of the seabed. It was harvested, dried and then burnt in stone kilns (there were at least 150 on Rathlin). It was heavy work: five tons of dry or ten tons of wet seaweed would result in a single ton of saleable 'ash'. This alkali was used in the manufacture of glass, soap and linen. At the start of the 19th century cheap imports of alkali from Spain (made by burning saltwort) threatened the kelp market, but thankfully a new discovery had been made – the ash was rich in iodine, a previously unknown element that had many medicinal uses. The discovery of penicillin and other sources for iodine finally killed off the industry in the 20th century.

Skellig Michael

Violently jutting out of the Atlantic, nine miles west of County Kerry, are Skellig Michael and nearby Little Skellig. A group of monks moved there, some time between the 6th and 8th centuries, and stayed until the 13th century: the remains of their monastery are still visible today. Looking like something from *Game of Thrones*, a path winds up the cliffs of Skellig Michael to a cluster of austere domed stone cells. In 1910 George Bernard Shaw wrote a wonderful letter describing a visit he had recently made...

'My Dear Jackson,
Yesterday I left the Kerry coast in an open boat, 33 feet long, propelled by ten men on five oars... they landed me on the most fantastic and impossible rock in the world: Skellig Michael, or the Great Skellig... Most incredible of all, the lighthouse keeper will not take a tip, but sits proud, melancholy and haunted in his kitchen after placing all his pantry at your disposal. He will also accompany you down to the desperate little harbour to squeeze the last word out of you before you abandon him...

I tell you the thing does not belong to any world that you and I have lived and worked in: it is part of our dream world. Then back in the dark, without compass, and the moon invisible in the mist, 49 strokes to the minute striking patines of white fire from the Atlantic, spurting across threatening currents, and furious tideraces, pursued by terrors, ghosts from Michael, possibilities of the sea rising making every fresh breeze a fresh fright, impossibilities of being quite sure whither we were heading, two hours and a half before us at best, all the rowers wildly imaginative, superstitious, excitable, and apparently super-human in energy and endurance...'
– 18 September 1910

Scottish Islands

64.

Ailsa Craig

Ailsa Craig is a somewhat unprepossessing little teardrop-shaped island approximately three-quarters of a mile long and half a mile wide, sited at the mouth of the Firth of Clyde south of Glasgow. It is known for its granite, specifically three types: Common Green, Blue Hone and Red Hone. The exclusive right to mine the granite is held by a sporting goods company, 'Kays of Scotland'. Every few years they remove up to 2,000 tonnes of it, ship it

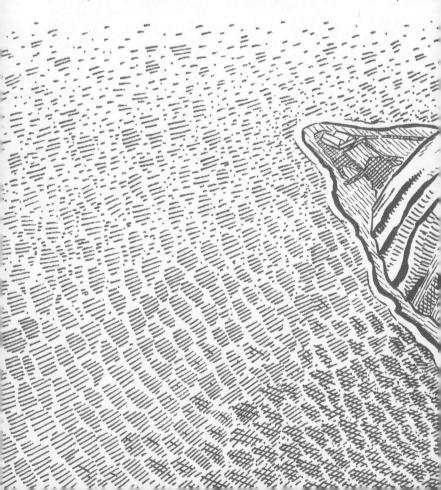

back to the mainland and turn it into curling stones that are exported round the world. They have been doing this since 1851.

It is also home to oversize slow worms – a case of island gigantism.

In environments where animals have no natural predators they often grow in size. Other examples include giant rats on the Indonesian island of Flores and the giant pill-millipede from Madagascar.

IF at first you don't succeed, try,
try again. This is the lesson Robert
the Bruce learned whilst hiding in
a cave from the English and watching
a spider repeatedly try and spin a web
on the wall of a cave. At least this is
what Sir Walter Scott in his book, *Tales
of a Grandfather*, attributed to the
Scottish leader. Such is the power
of a good story that a great deal of
energy has been devoted to discovering
the actual cave. There are at least
four suggested sites, including one on
Arran, the King's Cave.

Bass Rock

Looking like a large slice of cake lying on its side, Bass Rock lies at the mouth of the Firth of Forth facing the North Sea on Scotland's east coast. It contains a ruined castle and a chapel, evidence of its strategic importance over the centuries.

Landing on the rock is perilous but it is possible to sail through it. A 560-foot long tunnel cuts through the island from east to west. For a period its only inhabitants were lighthouse keepers, but automation made them redundant in the early 1980s.

Bell Rock

'Placed between hope and despair,
but certainly the latter was by much the
predominant feeling of his mind – situate
upon a sunken rock in the middle of the ocean,
which, in the progress of the flood-tide,
was to be laid under water to a depth of
at least 12 feet in a stormy sea. There were
this morning in all 32 persons on the rock, with
only two boats, whose complement, even in
good weather, did not exceed 24 sitters.'
From David Stevenson's *Life of Robert Stevenson*

Robert Stevenson was building a lighthouse
on Bell Rock (also known as Inch Cape),
a reef 12 miles east of Dundee, that peaks
3 feet above the waves at low tide, when
one of his boats broke free of its mooring.

He was left in a terrible predicament – the
tide was coming in and there was not enough
room in the remaining boats for all the men.
Resigned to their fate, the men stood in
silence. But fortune was on their side: a boat
carrying mail from Arbroath spotted the men
and came to their rescue. The lighthouse took
four years to build. Work on the rock could
only be undertaken during the summer months.
It was first illuminated in February 1811
and is still operating over 200 years later.
Legend has it that in the 14th century
the Abbot of Arbroath first commissioned
a floating bell on the rock that was tolled
by the action of the wind and the waves.

The Hebrides

Off the west coast of Scotland are the Hebrides. With a strong Celtic culture they have long been the inspiration for artists and writers. One of the foremost is the writer Compton Mackenzie. Although he was born in Hartlepool he was a livelong lover of islands.

In the early 1920s he rented and lived on two Channel Islands, Herm and Jethou, but he is best known for his relationship with Barra, an island in the Outer Hebrides. He moved there in 1928 and built a large house near the sea. Although he wasn't Scottish he identified closely with the country and its Gaelic culture, and was co-founder of the Scottish National Party. During his life he published over 100 books, including ten volumes of autobiography. His most famous works are the novels *Whisky Galore* (see page 87), *The Monarch of the Glen* and *Sinister Street*.

Mackenzie died in 1972, aged 89. His body was flown back to Barra and the plane was met by his friend Calum Johnson, an octogenarian piper. In driving rain and accompanied by a large number of mourners, Johnson piped the coffin up a steep slope to the cemetery. As the service finished, Johnson collapsed and died next to Mackenzie's grave: a dramatic ending that would not have been out of place in one of his books.

Colonsay

In 1995, archaeologists found hundreds
of thousands of roasted hazelnut shells in
a pit or midden, on the east coast of Colonsay.
Once dated they revealed that humans have
lived here for 9,000 years. Hazelnuts have been
found at other mesolithic sites but never in such
numbers. The purpose of the roasting is unclear
but probably it was to lengthen the time they
could be stored.

In 1882, erosion of sand dunes at Kiloran
Bay uncovered the remains of a Viking grave.
The man had been buried with his horse
and his possessions and then covered with
a 30-foot longboat. He had with him: an
axehead, a spearhead, a sword, a knife,
a buckle, a silver pin and some scales.
Nearby, two stone slabs with rough crosses
carved on them were found.

The curious stone figure opposite is the Riasg
Buidhe Cross, half man, half fish, dating back
to the 7th century. It is currently located
in the gardens of Colonsay House, having
been relocated from a chapel where it was
used among other things to cover a well.

In 2013 the local newspaper reported
on a rare incident of crime on Colonsay,
an act of vandalism after an alcohol-fuelled
argument. The reporter interviewed one of the
locals, who said, 'The last crime I heard of was
40 years ago and involved potatoes.'

Eilach An Naomih

One hundred and eighty nine lonely acres in the Inner Hebrides, this uninhabited island contains evidence of early Christian settlement; there is a ruined chapel, monastery, graveyard and a double beehive cell, possibly the earliest church buildings in Britain. It is believed that St Columba visited in the 6th century, founded a monastery and buried his mother Eithne there. It has also been identified as Ailech – one of the many monasteries set up by Brendan the Navigator before he set off on his trip to find the Fortunate Isles. Like other island monasteries in the 8th century it became vulnerable to Viking attack and was abandoned. More recently it has been used for grazing by farmers on neighbouring islands.

Eilean Bàn

In 1963, the aristocrat, naturalist and author Gavin Maxwell bought a pair of lighthouse keeper's cottages on the six-acre island of Eilean Bàn located between Skye and the Scottish mainland. He was flush from the success of *Ring of Bright Water*, his autobiographical account of caring for otters which sold millions of copies worldwide and would be made into a successful film. He eventually moved to Eilean Bàn in 1968 after a fire destroyed his old home at Sandraig.

It was not Maxwell's first island adventure. After working as a spy instructor in the Second World War he bought the island of Soay, also off Skye, and attempted to set up a business hunting basking sharks. His aim was to create the 'Island Valley of Avalon', albeit one with a lot more blubber and blood. He related the story of this ultimately failed venture in his 1952 book, *Harpoon at a Venture*.

His plan on Eilean Bàn was to set up a small zoo. Sadly he died only a year after moving there. His cottages are now the Bright Water Visitor Centre. The island, though, is not the place it was when Maxwell was alive. The giant concrete Skye Road Bridge now dominates, running right through the middle of the island. It is hard to imagine that it was ever a place of tranquility.

Eriskay

On 3 February 1941, the SS *Politician* left Liverpool carrying, among its cargo, 260,000 bottles of whisky. Two days later the ship was caught in a storm in the Western Isles and ran aground off the coast of Eriskay. Local islanders sailed out to rescue the crew. Once news spread of the whisky, many other boats arrived during the night to reclaim as many bottles as possible before the customs and excise men arrived.

Due to wartime rationing there had been little whisky available. It was believed 24,000 bottles were removed from the ship, much to the anger of the local customs officer Charles McColl. The writer Compton Mackenzie (see page 74) later used the story as the basis of his 1947 novel, *Whisky Galore*. In 1949, it was turned into a film by Ealing Studios starring Joan Greenwood, Gordon Jackson and Basil Radford.

A type of morning glory that only grows on Eriskay and nearby Vatersay, known as Bonnie Prince Charlie's flower, was purportedly brought to the islands as seeds from France by the Young Pretender and dropped on the beach by him when he landed in Eriskay on 25 July 1745. From here he gathered a Highland army to face the English crown. He enjoyed some success before he was eventually defeated at Culloden Moor. This was the last battle to be fought on British soil, and had far-reaching consequences. One was that it led to the end of the old clan system.

Flannan Isles

'It was with deep regret I wish you to learn the very sad affair that has taken place here during the past fortnight; namely the disappearance of my two fellow lightkeepers Mr Ducat and Mr Marshall, together with Occasional Keeper Donald McArthur from off this island.'
Mr Moore, Assistant Lightkeeper, December 1900

The Flannan Islands (also known as the Seven Hunters) are seven small islands 80 miles west of the Scottish mainland, and 20 miles west of Lewis. Between 1895 and 1899, and under the direction of Charles and David Stevenson, a lighthouse was built on one of the islands, Eilean Mor. A year after construction was finished disaster struck. On 26 December a boat arrived carrying the lighthouse keepers' relief. They discovered an eerie scene – an untouched meal on the table, an upturned chair, but no lighthouse keepers. There was much conjecture in the press. Had they murdered each other? Had they been taken away by the phantom of the Seven Hunters? The most likely explanation is that they were swept away by the sea, but no-one will ever know what happened that Christmas.

Jura

Jura is part of the Inner Hebrides, next to Islay, on the west coast of Scotland. It covers 142 square miles, much of this is bog. It is home to 200 people and 5,000 deer. Visiting in 1713, Martin Martin noted, 'The natives here are very well proportioned, being generally black of complexion and free from bodily imperfections. They speak the Irish language, and wear the plaid, bonnet, etc.' He also said he had been told of an islander living 'one hundred and eighty Christmasses'.

Orwell wrote *1984* whilst living in Barnhill, a remote cottage on Jura that he had been lent by his friend and benefactor Lord Astor (who also owned the *Observer*, which employed Orwell). He moved there in May 1946. It was not an easy time; his wife had recently died, leaving him a single parent. The cottage was simple, with no electricity, and Orwell had to bring a camp bed, chairs and a table with him. He soon moved in his sister Avril, along with his son and a nanny.

The isolation suited him, but the book was a struggle and he was constantly battling ill health, including a bout of TB. He delivered the manuscript at the end of 1948, it was published six months later and was quickly recognised as masterpiece, but Orwell's health was now failing. He died on 21 January 1949 in a sanatorium in the Cotswolds.

Lewis

Callanish is a remote and extraordinary circle of ancient stones on the west coast of Lewis. It consists of 13 stones up to 16 feet in height. The largest stands at the entrance to a burial chamber. There are avenues of smaller stones on the north, east, south and west sides that lead up to the central circle. It is believed that the purpose of Callanish was to mark when the moon was lowest in the sky, an event that happens every 18.61 years. Archaeologists have dated Callanish as

being 4–5,000 years old, though the burial chamber is more recent. In 800 BC the site was abandoned and gradually it became covered in peat. In 1695, Martin Martin visited the site and reported that the locals told him druids had used it in the past 'in the time of heathenism'. The stones were still largely buried until 1857, when the landowner James Matheson began cutting away five feet of peat to reveal their full glory.

Luchruban

Donald Munro's 1549 work, *Description of the Western Isles of Scotland*, is the first written account of a visit to the Hebrides. He states that the tidal island of Luchruban, off the north coast of Lewis, is also known as Pygmeis Isle, claiming that small human bones had been found buried there. Writing in the 17th century, Martin Martin repeats this notion, calling

Luchruban, 'The Island of Pigmies or the Island of the Little Men'. Needless to say, no evidence of the little people has ever been discovered. Tiny people or creatures have a long history in Scottish stories, with fairies making their first appearance in a 1450 poem about King Berdok who spent the summer in a cabbage stalk and the winter in a cockleshell.

Rum

George Bullough inherited a large portion of his father's fortune along with the island of Rum a few days before his 21st birthday. The vast amount of money he spent building and furnishing Kinloch Castle led to colourful rumours about his lifestyle and tastes.

It was said that he paid the 300 builders extra so they would wear kilts, and that he had been sent on a round-the-world cruise by his father after he caught him in bed with his stepmother. The latter is certainly untrue, but George did devote much of his time to travelling in a luxury yacht. And Kinloch Castle is over the top – turtles and alligators had their own special ponds, hummingbirds circled vines, peach and nectarine trees grew in the conservatory, bathrooms boasted showers that shot jets from ten directions, and guests were entertained by an Orchestrion – a kind of supercharged cinema organ that imitated a 40-piece orchestra.

Bullough and his family enjoyed hunting and fishing and entertained on a lavish scale. A bill for a party their daughter threw in 1926 when she was only 20 includes 169 bottles of champagne, 26 bottles of wine, 16 bottles of brandy and 3 bottles of port. Before Bullough's wife Monica died she sold the island to the Nature Conservancy (later called Scottish Natural Heritage) at a greatly reduced price.

Skye

Crofting was the traditional and most widespread form of agricultural activity carried out in the Scottish Highlands and islands. Typically the croft would consist of a simple house, a field to grow crops, and communally held land for animal grazing. The crofters often suffered at the hands of aristocratic absentee landlords who had assumed ownership of the land through the clan system. In the late 18th century the landlords realised they could make more money from sheep farming and began enclosing the common land and forcibly evicting their tenant farmers, many of whom were forced to emigrate.

On the Isle of Skye the crofters rebelled and refused to pay their rent. The laird responded by ordering their eviction.

Fifty police officers were dispatched to Skye to assist with the task. At Braes they were met by a barrage of missiles. A number of crofters were arrested. This led the government to act, and they set up a commission of inquiry in 1883. More rent strikes and disorder followed until the 1885 Crofter Act was passed, bringing some security of tenure to the crofters for the first time.

Old Man of Storr
Looking like a set of Obelix's menhirs, The Storr is a rocky ridge, the result of a giant landslip that pokes up from the hillside on the Isle of Skye. It is one of the best-known of all island landmarks and is visited by up to 50,000 people a year.

The largest rock in outline looks a little like a face, it is known as the Old Man. It was allegedly created by a brownie (a goblin-like creature popular in Scottish folk tales) commemorating O'Sheen, a local villager who had earlier saved the brownie's life.

Staffa

Half a mile long and a quarter of a mile wide, this uninhabited volcanic island in the southern Inner Hebrides is famous for its numerous caves and hexagonal basalt columns (also found on the Giant's Causeway and Rathlin Island in Ireland).

Its best-known feature is Fingal's Cave, which has provided inspiration for artists ever since the great naturalist Sir Joseph Banks visited in August 1772. The night before his visit he stayed at the house of the island's only inhabitants, where he became infested with lice. This didn't stop him later waxing lyrical about what he saw: 'In a short time we arrived at the mouth of the cave, the most magnificent, I supposed, that has ever been described by travellers. The mind can hardly form an idea more magnificent than such a place.'

In Gaelic it was called An Uaimh Bhinn, which means 'the melodious cave'. And it was the cave's eerie acoustics that led the composer Felix Mendelssohn to write an overture, *The Hebrides* (also known as *Fingal's Cave*), after visiting in 1829. Other famous tourists included Tennyson, Keats, Wordsworth, Turner, Sir Walter Scott, Jules Verne as well as Queen Victoria and Prince Albert. The cave's name is derived from the Irish hero Fingal, immortalised in James MacPherson's poetry.

James MacPherson

Born in 1736, James MacPherson was
a teacher and former student of King's
College, St Andrews. He wrote poetry while
he was studying and, after he left, began
collecting Gaelic verse and folklore. In 1760
he set off on a poetry collecting trip to Skye,
North Uist, South Uist and Benbecula (and
later the Isle of Mull). The following year he
claimed to have discovered an ancient epic
poem written in Gaelic in the 3rd century.

His translation was published as *Fingal,
an Ancient Epic Poem in Six Books, together
with Several Other Poems composed by Ossian,
the Son of Fingal.* It proved popular and was
soon translated into a number of languages;
admirers included Goethe and Napoleon,
and it is cited as one of catalysts of the
Romantic movement in Germany.

There were, however, some doubts at the
time about the authenticity of MacPherson's
sources. He never showed anyone the original
manuscripts, and now it is generally assumed
that he made lots of it up. Samuel Johnson,
who toured the Scottish Highlands and islands
in 1773, was a particularly vociferous critic.

The controversy did not do MacPherson
any long lasting damage. He went on to
become an MP, and eventually bought an
estate in Inverness-shire near his birthplace.

North Rona

Fifty miles west of Cape Wrath is the uninhabited island of North Rona. The writer and conservationist Frank Fraser Darling, along with his wife Bobbie and his eight-year-old son Alasdair, moved here in July 1938 to study grey seals. It was a rough-hewn existence, with the family staying in temporary sheds that Darling was never sure would survive the storms which were a regular feature of island life. He wrote a number of bestselling books about his time here and on the Summer Isles, that were widely read during the Second World War.

In 1969 he delivered the BBC Reith Lectures, a groundbreaking series of talks on ecology called 'Wilderness and Plenty', that reflected on man's responsibility to look after the planet. He defined ecology as being, 'a delight in knowing how nature works and a love of beauty that may or may not be conscious'.

Orkney Islands

St Magnus Cathedral

Ten miles off the north coast of Scotland
are 70 islands collectively known as the
Orkneys. They have a long history of human
habitation. The *Orkneyinga Saga*, a history
of the Orkney Islands, was written in about
1230. It tells how in the 11th century the
Norwegian King Magnus 'Barelegs' arrived
in Orkney and defeated the two ruling earls.
He then departed for a raid on Anglesey taking
with him the sons of the two earls: Hakon
and Magnus. As the Vikings attacked the
Welsh, Magnus (not the bare legs one) refused
to join in. He stayed on board the ship singing
psalms. This holy behaviour was not, however,
the reason why he became a saint.

The Orkneys were eventually restored
to Hakon and him but they started arguing.
A tentative peace was negotiated and it
was agreed they would meet on the island
of Egilsay, each bringing with them two ships.
Hakon brought eight ships and attacked and
killed Magnus. His grave at Birsay became
a place of pilgrimage after it was connected
to a number of miracles. He was canonised
in 1135 and work on the cathedral in Kirkwall
began in 1137.

It has its own dungeon known as Markwick's
Hole. Access to the dungeon was via a chute
in the Hall of Justice. Prisoners would
be pushed down it, then the top would be
covered and they would be left in darkness.

Stenness

The 100-foot-wide stone circle at Stenness on the Orkney Mainland is 5,000 years old. The largest stone is nearly 20 foot high. Evidence suggests that there were once twelve stones at one time, but there are only four left standing. They were surrounded by a circular ditch, 13 feet wide and beyond that an earth bank, which had a single entrance on the north side, but the bank and ditch are no longer visible. In the middle of the circle were two hearths. Animal bones and pottery found there suggests they were used for cooking. The Odin stone stood 460 feet to the north of the circle. It was eight feet in height and had a distinctive hole in its body. In 1814 it was destroyed by the leaseholder of the site, Captain W Mackay, because he was angered by the amount of visitors the stones attracted. The locals, in turn, were so annoyed by his actions that they tried to burn down his house. Eventually a local historian managed to get the law to intervene, but by then Mackay had broken up the Odin stone and another stone in the main circle.

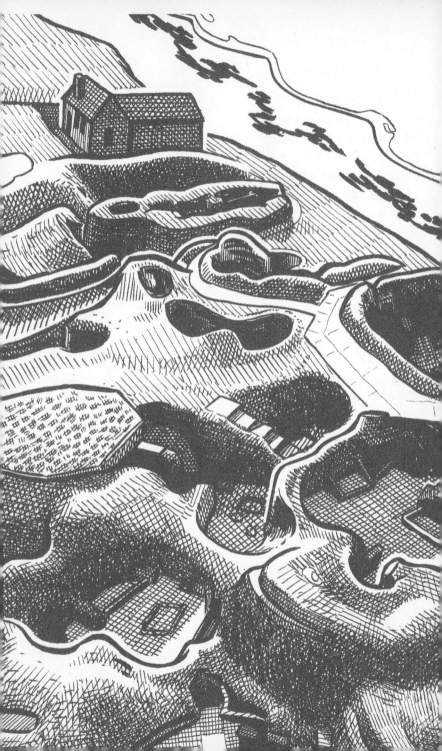

Skara Brae

In 1850, during a storm, high tides removed the grass from a small hill on the Orkney Mainland revealing the outlines of four stone houses. A small amount of excavation was done but it was not until another storm in 1925 that the full extent of this amazing neolithic settlement was revealed. There are eight houses, each containing stone beds and stone furniture, connected by low covered corridors. They were lived in for six hundred years at some point between four and five thousand years ago. Each has a square central room, with a fireplace flanked by two beds and a dresser on the wall opposite.

Scapa Flow

South of the Orkney Mainland is a 120-square-mile area of sea called Scapa Flow that has been used as a harbour since the Vikings arrived in the 8th century. In the First World War it became the main base for the Royal Navy. The German fleet of 74 ships was brought to Scapa Flow after they surrendered.

On 21 June 1919, mistakenly believing that peace negotiations had failed, Rear Admiral Ludwig von Reuter sent out a secret coded message, 'Paragraph eleven confirm'. The Germans sailors immediately set about scuttling the whole fleet. Remarkably, this giant sinking was witnessed by a party of schoolchildren on a boat trip, one of whom later described the scene: 'And as we watched, awestruck and silent, the sea became littered for miles round with boats and hammocks, lifebelts and chests, and among it all hundreds of men struggling for their lives.'

THE SMS CÖLN

Hoy

In July 1967 an astounding 15 million people tuned into the BBC show, *The Great Climb*, to watch live as a group of six mountaineers ascended the iconic 450-foot sea stack, The Old Man of Hoy. It was one of the most ambitious outside broadcasts ever attempted; 16 tons of equipment had to be brought to these remote cliffs, and for the last three miles everything had to be hauled across a roadless bog. In 2014 one of the original six, Chris Bonington, climbed the Old Man again, this time to mark his 80th birthday and raise money for charity. When thinking about the landscape it is easy to make the mistake of believing it has remained unchanged for millennia. A good example of why this is wrong is the Old Man, which broke free from the surrounding cliffs as recently as the early 19th century.

Papa Westray

Dating back to 3600 BC, the Knap Of Howar are the oldest standing buildings in Northern Europe. They are found on Papa Westray, an island 20 miles from the Orkney mainland that measures four miles by one mile. The dwellings consist of two chambers with a linking door. One side was used for living, and contains two spaces divided by stone slabs as well as a hearth and

other stone furniture, whilst the other side was used as a workshop. They were probably part of a farmstead and there is evidence to suggest they were not the first buildings on the site. There are over 60 archaeological sites on the island. Since 2009, three 5,000-year-old carved stone human figures have been found, each only a few centimetres in length.

Rockall

The final expansion of the British empire took place on 18 September, 1955 on a barren outcrop of granite the size of a small office block that lies in the Atlantic between Iceland, Ireland and Scotland. Three naval officers and the naturalist James Fisher were dropped by helicopter onto its summit. They raised a Union flag and cemented a plaque to the rock that declared Rockall was now part of Britain. This ceremony was driven by a fear that

the Russians might place surveillance equipment there. Eighteen years later the UK parliament passed The Island of Rockall Act, incorporating it into Scotland (although it is 19 miles nearer Ireland). Rockall was now officially an island. This upgrade was driven by economics. The government felt it would improve their claim to any oil finds in the seabed. Since the 1980s Denmark, Iceland and Ireland have all disputed the legality of the Act.

Shetland Isles

On the shore at Scalloway 50 miles north of the Orkneys is the Shetland archipelago. They are closer to Norway than London. This proximity is reflected in their culture and history. Scalloway on the largest island, known as Mainland, has a war memorial commemorating the men who lost their lives operating the 'Shetland Bus'. On 9 April 1940 Germany invaded Norway, starting an exodus of Norwegians to the Shetlands.

With help from the Royal Navy these expats began organising trips back to Norway, dropping supplies and men to help the resistance movement. Originally these journeys were made in fishing boats, as it was believed the Germans would not be able to identify them among the regular fishing fleet, but eventually the Germans realised what was going on and required all vessels to carry passes and not stray from coastal waters. In 1943 the Americans stepped in to help by supplying three submarine chasers that were able to sail at far greater speed. By the end of the war the 'Shetland Bus' had carried 192 agents and 383 tons of weapons into Norway.

In the South Seas
John Clunies-Ross was
born in Weisdale on the
Shetland Mainland in
1786. In his thirties he left
Scotland and travelled to
the Cocos Islands,
a tropical paradise in
the Indian Ocean midway
between Australia and Sri
Lanka. He began a business
selling copra, the dried

JOHN CLUNIES ROSS

flesh of the coconut. Using Malay workers, he lived like a feudal lord in a large house on Home Island. He paid staff with a currency that he minted which was only redeemable in the islands' shop, which he owned.

A hundred years and a few generations later, Queen Victoria granted the islands to the Clunies-Ross family. This situation carried on until 1978 when the family was forced to sell to the Australian government for £2.5 million. About 350 descendants of the original workers and a member of the Clunies-Ross family remain on the islands (but he is no longer in the stately old family home, Oceania House).

Writers that visited the South Sea islands in the 19th century helped create a romantic myth of them as a version of paradise.

Herman Melville, the author of *Moby Dick*, travelled to Polynesia in 1842 and four years later had a bestseller with *Typee*, a book about his experiences. Robert Louis Stevenson, author of *Treasure Island* and *Kidnapped* (and descendant of the famous Scottish family of lighthouse builders), sailed around the Pacific in 1888 and wrote *In the South Seas*. A few years later he bought a plot of land in Samoa and built a house. He died there in 1894.

Sullom Voe

Following international negotiations, the Continental Shelf Act was passed in 1964. It set out which areas of the ocean bed could be exploited by the UK. A year later BP's first rig, the *Sea Gem*, struck oil in the North Sea, although not enough for commercial exploitation. The really big discoveries took place at the start of the 1970s. Sullom Voe, on Northern Mainland, was built to process oil and gas from the Brent oilfield and today is one of the largest refineries in Europe.

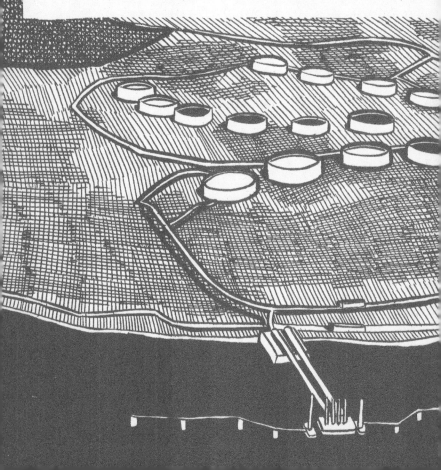

It occupies a 1,000 acre site, roughly the size of 550 football pitches, and is a vital element in the Shetland economy. Since opening in the early 1970s it has processed over 8 billion barrels of oil, roughly a third of the total produced across all North Sea fields.

Brent is named after the Brent goose. There is an apocryphal story that Shell were going to name their first field A UK, until someone realised that this would inevitably lead to F UK, so they changed policy and decided to name their oilfields after birds.

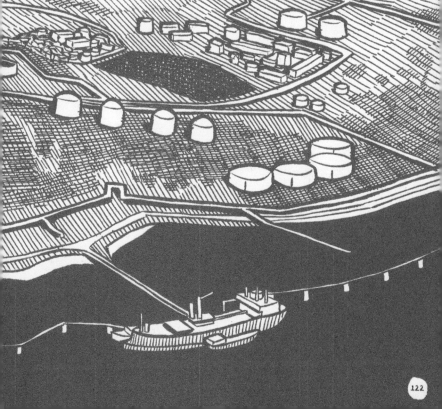

Fair Isle

Halfway between the Orkneys and Shetland, with a population of around 80, is Fair Isle, three and a half miles long and one and half miles wide. It is famous for its shipwrecks, its birdlife and its colourful geometric patterned jumpers. After the Armada in 1588 the English chased the beaten Spanish fleet north. Their flagship *El Gran Grifon* was wrecked on Fair Isle. The 200 survivors were made welcome, but soon became a drain on the island's resources. According to the 19th-century folklorist Walter Traill Dennison, any Spaniard found alone was shoved

off the nearest cliff.
An Edinburgh bookseller,
George Waterson, planned
the original bird observatory
while imprisoned with a
group of keen ornithologists
in Germany during the
Second World War. When
he was repatriated the
first land he saw was Fair
Isle, and in 1947 he bought
the island and set up the
first observatory in some
old military huts.

124

Foula

The most westerly island in the Shetlands is Foula, lying 14 miles from Mainland. It only adopted Scottish law in the late 17th century. Norn, a language once used throughout the Shetlands and the Orkneys, was spoken on Foula (and Unst) later than anywhere else – until the early 19th century. Other Norse traditions still in evidence include celebrating Christmas and New Year using the old Julian calendar (the rest of the UK swapped to the Gregorian calendar in 1752). Yule is on 6 January and Newerday on 13 January. Its cliffs are the second highest in the UK after St Kilda. The filmmaker Michael Powell spent the summer of 1936 on Foula shooting the feature film, *Edge of the World*. Using local people as actors, the story was loosely based on the evacuation of St Kilda, and it conveys a vivid sense of the power of the sea over life in this wild place.

Outstack & Muckle Flugga

Out stack is a dark grey hump lying a few hundred yards off the coast of the uninhabited island of Muckle Flugga in the Shetlands. It is the northernmost point of the British Isles. These two islands supposedly appeared after two giants, Saxa and Herma, fighting over the love of a mermaid, hurled large stones at each other. It is nearer to Denmark, Iceland, Norway and Sweden than it is to London. The lighthouse on Muckle Flugga was built in 1854. It was an amazing feat of engineering – 120 tonnes of stone, cement and tools were carried by hand up 200-foot cliffs. A barracks was constructed on the summit and this became home to 20 men. Work started on 31 July 1854 and a temporary lighthouse was in place by 11 October. After much argument it was replaced by a more permanent structure. The one big change was that the new lighthouse was made of brick, not stone; bricks being far easier to transport. The lighthouse is still standing.

'A dozen cutlasses selected hastily from an arm chest and whose rusted hue bespoke how seldom they left the sheath armed the same number of young Zetlanders with whom mingled six maidens led by Minna Troil, and the minstrelsy instantly commenced a tune appropriate to the ancient Norwegian war-dance, the evolutions of which are perhaps still practised in those remote islands. The first movement was graceful and majestic, the youths holding their swords erect, and without much gesture; but the tune and the corresponding motions of the dancers, became gradually more and more rapid...'

This is how Sir Walter Scott described sword dancing on Papa Stour in his 1831 novel, *The Pirate*. No-one really knows how far the tradition dates back, but the earliest mention of a 'war-dance' in Scotland is from the 15th-century chronicle, *The Scotichronicon*, by Walter Bower. In June 2008, a tiny isle, off the coast of Papa Stour, was declared independent. Stuart Hill was making a serious point: the Shetlands were never legally passed over to the Scottish crown after they were pawned and then forfeited by the Danish royal family in 1469. This point was rather lost in the media storm that carried the story round the world. Mr Hill, originally from Suffolk, was in Shetland after being rescued (for the eighth time) in an attempt to sail round the British Isles in a 14-foot boat.

Whalsay

Before the European Union was a twinkle in a Brussels bureaucrat's eye there was another federation that promoted trading relationships across the continent. The Hanseatic League was formed by city merchants across northern Europe as a way of protecting their interests when moving goods.

It started in the mid 13th century and at its height consisted of 170 cities that stretched through Belgium, Germany, Poland, Russia and Latvia. While the league was keen to promote free trade between its members, it had a highly protectionist stance against outsiders. In 1368 the league blockaded Norwegian ports to stop grain imports, forcing the authorities to give them trade privileges not enjoyed by other countries. When their interests were under threat they also funded military action. In 1370 70 Hanseatic cities contributed to a war with King Valdema of Denmark, who had attacked the Swedish city of Visby because he was angry about the league's trade restrictions.

In 1356 the Hansa cities formed a parliament known as the Diet, but the league never seemed to be able to agree on anything for long. In countries that were not part of the league they established 'kontors' or trading posts. There were a number in the UK, the most famous being the Steelyard in London, but there was also one at Symbister on Whalsay (it is now a small museum). The league were important trading partners to the whole of the Shetlands, buying salted fish in return for cloth, seeds, salt and iron. This lasted until the Act of the Union in 1707 that banned German merchants.

Yell

Yell is one of the most northern Shetland Islands. This statue of a woman and child looking out to sea was erected on the 100th anniversary of the Gloup fishing disaster, when ten boats from Yell were lost.

The families of those who died faced poverty and a relief committee was formed. This is an extract of their first report printed in December 1881... 'On the night of Wednesday the 20th July, 1881, the whole of the haaf fleet belonging to the North Isles was at sea. The day had been fine and the air warm. Some heavy showers had fallen towards evening, but except for a heavy swell on the sea, supposed to have been caused by the rain, there were no indications of an approaching storm... Most of the boats were forty to sixty miles out at sea, when all at once, and without any warning... a violent storm from the north-west broke upon them. Between midnight and one o'clock A.M. on Thursday, the gale was at its height. About the latter hour it commenced gradually to moderate. So suddenly had wind and sea arisen that some of the crews had not time to reef their sails, and had to set them for land just as they were. Thus over-rigged, they staggered and plunged onwards.'

Fifty-eight men died that night, although only seven bodies were ever recovered. They left behind eighty-five orphans and thirty-four widows. Thirty six of the dead came from the small village of Gloup.

St Kilda

St Kilda is a group of lonely islands, situated 50 miles west of the Outer Hebrides. People have lived here for over 2,000 years, but life has always been difficult, as St Kilda can be cut off from the rest of the world for months at a time.

The population had never been higher than 200, but by 1930 it had shrunk to just 36. Facing continuing food shortages and lack of medical help they wrote to the Secretary of State for Scotland and asked to be evacuated.

On 29 August 1931 two boats arrived and took them away. Many were given jobs with the Forestry Commission – a strange choice as St Kilda has no trees. Today the islands aren't completely deserted; there is a small military base on Hirta, and a constant trickle of visitors attracted by the bird life and the ghostly remains of a unique culture.

The Great Auk

In 1840 three men set off on a hunting trip
to Stac-an-Armin. Here they discovered
a bird they had never seen before. Black and
white, the size of a goose and without wings,
they realised it was the famed Great Auk, at
one time a regular summer visitor to St Kilda.
They caught the bird and took it back to their
hut. Bad weather set in and they were unable
to return home. Deeply superstitious, they
decided the auk was responsible for the storm
and beat it to death, dumping the body behind
the bothy. This was the last recorded sighting
of a Great Auk in the UK, and the second
last in the world. Today St Kilda is one of
the most important seabird stations in the
North Atlantic, with over a million seabirds
visiting between early spring and late autumn.
Gannets, puffins, guillemots and fulmars are
in particular abundance.

Rising to an awesome 300 feet, St Kilda has
the highest sea cliffs in Europe. The islanders
were expert climbers, lowering themselves
down terrifying sheer drops on home-made
horsehair ropes to trap seabirds, using long
poles with snares on the end. In the late 19th
century the pioneering naturalists the Keartons
photographed the thick, overdeveloped ankles
of the St Kildans, who preferred to climb
barefoot. For centuries the seabirds provided
the islanders with their staple diet: each adult
ate over 100 fulmars a year.

Ghost Village

You can still see the crescent of drystone houses on Hirta that were built in the 18th century. It was here each morning that the men met for the 'parliament', where work was divided up and any disputes were settled. Life on St Kilda was pre-industrial – people didn't have money, wear shoes, or even use toilets. They spoke Gaelic and dressed in homespun clothes. In 1931 two-thirds of the population were called Gillies or MacKinnon.

The island was owned by a distant landlord, whose boat came twice a year to deliver supplies and collect the rent that was paid in feathers and birds. Martin Martin, visiting in 1703, wrote that the St Kildans were 'happier than the generality of mankind as being almost the only people in the world who feel the sweetness of true liberty'. In the mid 19th century tourist boats began to arrive, bringing much needed income but also influenza and other fatal diseases.

One of the most iconic features on St Kilda are the 1,400 cleats, small domed storehouses, that randomly dot the landscape. Built of stone and with turf roofs, they are waterproof but not windproof – to aid drying. They were used to store tools, dead birds and newly born lambs. No-one knows their age but it estimated that they are over a thousand years old.

Welsh Islands

Anglesey
Bardsey
Caldey
Puffin Island
Ramsey
Skokholm

Anglesey

There is evidence from the 1st century Roman author Tacitus that Anglesey was a centre for druidism. He described a battle in which the Britons wore black robes, had dishevelled hair and held burning torches, while crazed women moved between the soldiers. Next to them a circle of druids shouted incantations to the heavens. The Romans at first were paralysed with fear, but then, deciding that they could

not be beaten by a group of lunatics (and women), they attacked and killed the lot. Afterwards they destroyed the druids' sacred groves – gruesome places with altars apparently draped in bloody entrails from human sacrifice. Medieval Welsh manuscripts claim that Anglesey was once part of mainland Wales; it is now separated by the Menai Straits. It is home to 70,000 people, only a few of whom claim to be druids.

Bardsey

After St Cadfan built a monastery
on Bardsey in the 6th century, it became
a place of pilgrimage known as the island
of 20,000 saints. It was said that three trips
to Bardsey were worth one trip to Rome.
After the Dissolution of the Monasteries
in 1537 it became a refuge for pirates.
This carried on until a fishing and farming
community was established in the 18th century.

In the early 19th century the first King of
Bardsey was appointed. The final King was
Love Pritchard, born in 1842. The archaeologist
Sir Mortimer Wheeler reported an encounter
with him in a pub: 'Against the bar was leaning
an old salt, with a mahogany face framed
in whiskers. Then to our "good morning"
he vouchsafed a grunt. Then, after a long
lapse, he spoke slowly in a rather gruff
Caernarvonshire singsong "Where dit we come
from?" I rashly ventured "Cardiff". The fog
thickened during another long pause, and then
from the whiskers came the terse sentiment
"All sorts comes from Cardiff" followed by
a skillful expectoration towards the door...
The postman leaned over the bar: "That
was the new King of Bardsey," he said, "he
does not much like foreigners."' Pritchard
offered his services to the Army during
The First World War but he was turned down
– he was 72. He took this as a terrible insult
and declared that from then on Bardsey would
be a neutral territory.

Caldey

With seven unspoilt sandy beaches, Caldey is far more welcoming than most neighbouring Welsh islands. It has been the home to monks since the 6th century. They are currently Cistercians that came from Chimay in Belgium in the 1920s, replacing a community of Benedictines who were led into a financial crisis by their colourful abbot Dom Aelred, a man fond of first-class travel and chauffeur-driven cars. He is not the first religious man associated with Caldey to have behaved in a questionable manner – in the 6th century the abbot St Pyr died after falling down the well while drunk.

Puffin Island

'Puffin Island is such a funny place, about half a mile long, and on all sides but one very steep and craggy. It is covered with lovely bright-coloured grass, and in the middle is an old tower, which is the relic of some monastery, but so old that nobody knows anything of its history. There were some sheep and rabbits feeding on the island, and oh! such lots of birds!'
Matilda Betham-Edwards, travel writer, 1860

Off the coast of Anglesey is the 69-acre Puffin Island. Thousands of puffins used to breed here, but the accidental introduction of rats in the 19th century decimated the population. A recent programme has now wiped out the rodents, and puffins are once more breeding here, but in very small numbers.

There are four species of puffin, the one found in the UK being the Atlantic puffin, identifiable by the blue triangle on its beak. They can fly at speeds up to 55 mph, achieved by beating their wings 400 times a minute. Between April and August they live in three-foot-long burrows. For the rest of the year they stay at sea, living on fish and drinking sea water. Using their wings to propel them, they are expert divers. Their beaks can carry lots of fish – the most recorded is 60. They can live up to 20 years, and start breeding at the age of five, laying a single egg per year.

Justinian, a Breton monk, established
a hermitage on Ramsey, a 640-acre island
off the far south-western edge of Wales
in the 6th century. When St David visited
he was impressed by Justinian's simple life
(St David believed people should live on water
and bread). He asked Justinian to become his
confessor and abbot at St David's Cathedral.
Justinian moved there for a few years before
eventually returning to the island. Sadly it was
not a happy ending. He was martyred by three
of his servants, who decapitated him. However,
this was not the end of Justinian. Firstly,
a spring burst up from where he lay, then his
corpse stood up, picked up his head and walked
over the sea to the mainland. His remains
were interred in the same tomb as St David.
His attackers were struck down with leprosy;
divine retribution perhaps.

Off the east coast is The Bitches, a run of
vicious-looking rocks that create a powerful
current particularly with the spring tides.
Legend has it that Justinian created them
while attempting to cut off Ramsey from the
indulgent, sinful mainland. Using an axe he
chopped at the land until his tool became
blunt, stopping him from finishing the job.

In the 1990s Ramsey was sold to the RSPB.
The coastline has high cliffs that provide
a perfect habitat for breeding seabirds.

Skokholm

In 1927, at the age of 24, Ronald Lockley
and his wife moved to the 240-acre uninhabited
(except for a lighthouse) island of Skokholm,
off the south-west coast of Wales. There
was just a ruined farmhouse with no roof,
but Lockley wasn't put off. His idea was to fish,
keep sheep and eat the rabbits, and alongside
this he planned to study birds, specifically the
shearwater and the storm petrel. A schooner,
the *Alice Williams*, ran aground and started
breaking up three months after they arrived.
Ronald bought the boat as salvage and rescued
40 tonnes of coal and a large quantity of wood,
which he used to renovate the farmhouse.
He started writing a column for *The Countryman*
magazine and then in 1930 published his first
book, *Dream Island: A record of a simple life*.

In 1933 he organised the first British Bird
Observatory on Skokholm. Lockley and his wife
had to leave the island when the army took
it over at the start of The Second World War.
During it he worked in naval intelligence and
afterwards moved to Orielton, a large estate
in Pembrokeshire where he studied rabbits.
This resulted in the book, *The Private Life
of the Rabbit*, that Richard Adams cited as
an inspiration for *Watership Down*. In 1970 he
moved to New Zealand to be near his daughter.
He carried on writing books about birds, whales,
nature and island life. By the time of his death
on 12 April 2000 he had written over 50 books.

Islands of the Imagination

Avalon

Doggerland

Hy Brazil

Kirrin Island

Sodor

Summerisle

Tír na nÓg

Utopia

Avalon first appears in Geoffrey of Monmouth's multi-volume pseudo-historical *History of the Kings of Britain,* that was published in 1136. It is mentioned twice. Firstly, as the place where King Arthur's sword was forged and, secondly, as the place he was taken to after he died to 'be cured of his wounds'.

Avalon is a classic Otherworld, one of the magical realms located on earth that regularly appear in medieval literature. Typically, they are islands containing apple trees, ruled over by women, where no-one gets old or ill.

Geoffrey also writes about Avalon in his later work, *The Life of Merlin,* but he changes its name from Insula Avallonis to Insula Pomorum (or the isle of apples). He explains that the injured Arthur was looked after by the fairy queen Morgan Le Fay and her nine sisters.

Since then the story has been re-told hundreds of times. The best known versions include Sir Thomas Mallorys 15th-century *Le Morte d'Arthur,* Tennyson's poem, *Idylls of the King,* and more recently, Marion Zimmer Bradley's novel *The Mists of Avalon.*

For an idea whose original written source is so slight, Avalon has done a remarkable job of capturing people's imagination for such a long period of time.

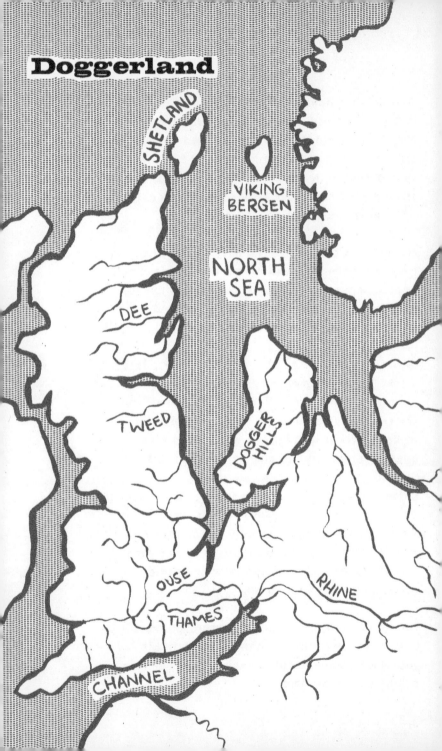

'We were halfway between the two north buoys in mid-channel between Leman and Ower... I heard the shovel strike something. I thought it was steel. I bent down and took it below. It lay in the middle of the block which was about four feet square and three feet deep. I wiped it clean and saw an object quite black.'
Pilgrim Lockwood,
captain of the trawler *Colinda*

The object Lockwood discovered, that night in September 1931, was a harpoon made of animal bone. It measured a little over eight inches long and was eventually dated as being approximately 13,000 years old.

'Moorlog' was the name fisherman gave to the blocks of peat that they often dredged up in their nets when trawling the bottom of the sea on the Dogger Bank, an area located halfway between the east coast of England and the Continent.

What made the harpoon special was, firstly, where it was found, 25 miles from the current British coast, and secondly, that it was encased in peat – it couldn't have been dropped from a boat; it had to have come from the time when this area was not covered by water. It was the first proof that people had lived there.

Our current coastline is the result of ice melting and sea rising when the last ice age finally ended 6,500 years ago. The biggest change was on our east coast: we were joined to the European mainland for a long time. Scientists believe that since 18,000 BC sea levels have risen as much as 400 feet (more than the height of St Paul's Cathedral).

Using seismic data from oil companies a picture has begun to emerge of this lost landscape. We know the Thames would have run directly into the Rhine, but as the sea rose a new landscape started forming. Around 5,500 BC the English Channel would have met the North Sea.

Soon after that Doggerland would have turned into an archipelago containing many islands. You could have travelled to the continent without losing sight of land, using them as stepping stones. But these islands and their communities did not last long.

Around 6,100 BC there was a dramatic submarine landslip. An area the size of Scotland collapsed into the North Sea. With waves travelling 70-100 feet per second the Storrega tsunamis would have devastated all coastal communities. Doggerland was no more.

Hy Brazil

The island of Hy Brazil first appeared on maps in the 13th century and survived cartographically right up until the mid 19th century; an impressive lifespan for a place that never existed. Lying south-west of Ireland, it was always drawn in a strangely symmetrical fashion as two half circles with an east-west sea passage running between them.

Its name is possibly derived from the Celtic word 'braes' meaning fortunate, and early reports clearly place it in the magical realm of other mythic Fortunate Islands (see Tír na nóg, page 173), it was reputedly continually shrouded in fog and had a tendency to disappear when ships sailed too close.

In 1480 a ship of 80 tonnes left Bristol with the purpose of sailing to Hy Brazil. The next year two ships, the *Trinity* and the *George* set out on the same unsuccessful search from the same port. The year 1498 saw the largest expedition yet, when John Cabot set off with five ships and 300 men. In the 17th century a number of people reported that they had seen or even visited the island.

In 1675 William Hamilton claimed that a Captain Nisbet of County Donegal had landed on Hy Brazil and lit a fire on the beach. This broke an enchantment and thereby freed a group of men who had been locked in a castle by a diabolical necromancer. The last reported sighting was in 1872, when TJ Westrop described the following scene: 'A dark island suddenly appeared far out to sea, but not on the horizon. It had two hills, one wooded; between them, from a low plain, rose towers and curls of smoke.' Although there is no evidence for Hy Brazil ever existing, some areas of the Atlantic were once dry land. It's said when St Lô visited the Channel Islands in 565 he could walk there across planks from France, and that they remained connected until 709.

Kirrin Island

Five on a Treasure Island, published in 1942, was the first of Enid Blyton's Famous Five books. The 'Five' in the title are a group of four friends (and a dog, Timmy) that spend their summers together getting caught up in a series of adventures, often featuring Kirrin Island and its ruined castle. Blyton wrote 21 Famous Five books. They have sold millions of copies and are still popular today.

The setting for Kirrin Island is somewhere off the Dorset coast, an area Blyton discovered in the 1930s, but the inspiration came from elsewhere. She wrote in a letter, 'It was an island I once visited several times when I was in Jersey, it lay off the coast and could only be reached either by boat or by a rocky path exposed when the tide was out. It had an old castle there and I longed to put the island and castle into a book. So I did, as you know!'

The parents of George, the girl who 'had always wanted to be a boy', own Kirrin, and have promised it will be hers when she is older. It provides the starting point for many stories: there are kidnaps, hidden tunnels, treasure maps, and in my favourite, *Five on Kirrin Island Again*, Uncle Quentin moves to the island for a whole summer to conduct secret experiments for the government and goes a bit barmy in the process.

Sodor

Thomas the Tank Engine lives on Sodor, a fictional island somewhere near the Isle of Man. Written by Rev. W Awdry, the railway series of children's books were first published in 1946.

The bishop on the Isle of Man still has the official title of 'Bishop of Sodor and Man'. Sodor is a reference to the time when Man was part of a kingdom that included the Hebrides. Awdry spotted this and, realising that Sodor no longer existed, borrowed the name. He took great pleasure in imagining Sodor, drawing detailed maps and writing a lengthy history that closely mimics the real history of many of the islands found in this book. It traces Sodor's past, from cursory visits by the Romans to monastic and saintly visitations (including a stop-off by St Brendan), attack and settlement by Vikings, through battles with the

Normans, right up to the present day. A playful thread of humour is weaved throughout: the publisher of a supposed four-volume *History of Sodor* is listed as Chatter and Windows (a play on the name of the publisher Chatto and Windus). This 'standard' work is attributed to Canon Dreswick (there is a Dreswick Point on the Isle of Man), who wrote it at Conk Abbey while recovering from a severe illness.

Awdry wrote a glossary of words in 'Sudric', a dying Gaelic language spoken on Sodor. Railways arrived in Sodor in 1806, and after that Awdry gets carried away listing each development in great detail. Awdry's enjoyment of writing about Sodor was an extension of the pleasure people get from playing with train sets or making model worlds: miniature kingdoms where they are in complete control.

Summerisle

Starring Christopher Lee
and Edward Woodward,
the 1973 cult film, *The
Wicker Man*, was set
on the fictional island
of Summerisle, located
somewhere off the west
coast of Scotland. There
is an actual group of
Scottish islands called
the Summer Isles but
they are not connected.

The story follows Sergeant
Howie, a policeman from
the mainland, who is sent

to Summerisle to find
a missing child. He soon
discovers that the
islanders, rather than
following Christianity,
worship the 'old gods'.

As his investigation
proceeds he is surprised
by a lack of co-operation
he receives from the
islanders and begins to
realise that something
quite different is going on.

It is hard to overestimate
the influence this sinister
film has had in shaping
contemporary ideas of
British islands (and the
countryside in general).
It contains lots of sexual
imagery; women dance
naked in Lord Summerisle's
garden, and Britt Eckland
strips in a room above
the island pub (the Green
Man). This fusing of
nature, paganism and
folk culture with sex
has proved to be a very
potent combination.

Tír na nÓg

There is a strand of Irish mythology in which a hero travels on a fantastic voyage to the 'blessed' or 'fortunate' isles. They are places of eternal youth, eternal summer and eternal love – a bit like the world of Beach Boys' songs. These stories are known as 'immrams' or sea sagas. They are all quite similar and often have interconnected elements. They often, as in *The Voyage of St Brendan*, incorporate Christian themes.

Tír na nÓg appears in a story about the poet and warrior Oisin. Niamh of the Golden Hair, the daughter of the sea god Manannan Mac Lir hears about Oisin and goes to visit him. They fall in love and she persuades him to return to her magical land Tír na nÓg. Eventually Oisin becomes homesick, Niamh lends him a white horse that can fly across the ocean, but warns he must never dismount. Arriving in Ireland he discovers that hundreds of years have passed and everything he held dear has gone. Distressed, and forgetting Niamh's warning, he jumps down off the horse, rapidly ages and dies.

In an age where the sea was the principal means of long distance travel it is not surprising that islands feature so heavily in these stories.

The narrative of leaving home in search of a better life, then being drawn back through homesickness, only to discover that home isn't how you remembered it, is a universal story as relevant now as it was then.

Thomas More's *Utopia* was a fictional account of an idealised island society, first published in Latin in 1516. It was not published in English until 1551, sixteen years after More's execution. By making it fictional, More was able to explore ideas of democracy, republicanism and atheism that would have otherwise landed him in trouble. There is no Christianity on Utopia; instead citizens are encouraged to be tolerant of all religious ideas and encouraged to choose between worshipping the sun, the moon, their ancestors, the planets or a single god.

The island is crescent-shaped and 200 miles across in the middle. There are 54 cities; the capital is Amaurot, chosen for its convenient location in the middle of the island. There is no private property, and no lock on any door. Each house has two slaves, who are forced to wear gold chains to show that wealth is of no importance. Food is taken communally and there are free hospitals. Women must confess their sins to their husbands once a month. There are no pubs. Gambling and hunting are discouraged.

More set *Utopia* on an island because it offered a framework around which he could build something distinct and complete – he didn't need to describe its neighbouring lands or its relation to the rest of the world.

Further Reading

A Description of the Western Islands of Scotland by Martin Martin. You can find digitised versions of this amazing early 18th-century book online.

Dream Island: a record of the simple life by Ronald Lockley. His first book about Skokholm.

Island Years, Island Farm by Frank Fraser Darling. This has recently been republished by the good folk at Little Toller.

Islands by RJ Berry. Masterful book in the Collins New Naturalist series.

The Lighthouse Stevensons by Bella Bathhurst. Great if you want to know more about the famous lighthouse builders.

The Maggie by James Dillon White. As good as *Whisky Galore* but not as well known. It was also made into an Ealing comedy.

www.theislandreview.com – Great online magazine for island lovers.

The Sea Kingdoms: The History of Celtic Britain and Ireland by Alistair Moffat. This will change the way you think about our national identity.

Further Listening

This list has been kindly supplied by Mathew's cousin, Danny Kilbride from Rag Foundation, www.ragfoundation.co.uk

Anglesey and Bardsey: Llio Rhydderch's *Enlli*
– www.lliorhydderch.com

Barry Island: Taran's *Catraeth*
– www.ynysrecords.com

Caldey Island: The Kilbride Brothers' *Sidan*

Hebrides: Mairi Smith's *Sgiath Airgid*

Isle of Lewis: Martyn Bennett
– www.martynbennett.com

Isle of Man: Barrule
– www.barruletrio.com

Lindisfarne: Alistair Anderson's
A Lindisfarne Gospel

Orkney Islands: Jennifer & Hazel Wrigley's
Huldreland

Shetland Islands: Tom Anderson's
The Silver Bow

Sully Island: The Root Doctors' *On the Wander*
– www.rootdoctors.co.uk

Acknowledgements

From Anthony...
With thanks to my family and friends for
their indispensable patience and support,
in particular auntie Gail and the Scott family
(Isle of Arran) and auntie Sally and the Hill
family (Isle of Wight) for fostering my love
of islands.

From Mathew...
I would like to thank everyone that has
encouraged and supported this project so
far: Jeff Barrett, Andrew Walsh, Robin Turner,
John Andrews, Carl Gosling, Danny Mitchell,
Catherine and Peregrine St Germans, Becky
Fincham, Nina Hervé, Sally Mesner Lyons, Carl
Mesner Lyons, Joseph Piercy, David Bramwell,
Ian and Clare Clayton, Ewan Clayton, Danny
Kilbride, Jenny Kilbride, everyone at Unbound,
the Crow's Nest crew and, of course, my
wonderful family Gemma, Laurie and Stella.

From both of us...
Our agent Diana Beaumont (not a resident
of Sark), Andrew Goodfellow, Anna Mrowiec,
everyone at Ebury, Ruth Killick.

This book was made possible with help
from the following amazing libraries:
Jubilee Library, Brighton, Lewes Library
and University of Sussex Library, Falmer.